All the Reasons
to Trust
Donald Trump

Bill Yancey

Front and Back Covers
by
Picture Perfect Cover Art
St. Augustine, FL

All the Reasons to Trust Donald Trump
Bill Yancey
© Copyright 2017 by Bill Yancey

Yancey, Bill, 1947—
Abandoned / Bill Yancey
ISBN-13: 978-1544624099
ISBN-10:154462093

1. Humor – Fiction 2. Political—Fiction 3. Fiction 4. Political Science
5. Politics and Social Studies

DEDICATION

TO ALL THE POLITICIANS IN THE USA

Also by Bill Yancey

Elvis Saves
No One Lives Forever
The Last Day
What Your Doctor Won't Tell You About Your Lower Back
Invictus
Multidimensional Man
Reluctant Intern
Deadly Practice
Quantum Timeline
Abandoned: MIA in Vietnam

Acknowledgements

Mark Twain for this quote:

Look at the tyranny of party -- at what is called party allegiance, party loyalty -- a snare invented by designing men for selfish purposes -- and which turns voters into chattles, slaves, rabbits, and all the while their masters, and they themselves are shouting rubbish about liberty, independence, freedom of opinion, freedom of speech, honestly unconscious of the fantastic contradiction; and forgetting or ignoring that their fathers and the churches shouted the same blasphemies a generation earlier when they were closing their doors against the hunted slave, beating his handful of humane defenders with Bible texts and billies, and pocketing the insults and licking the shoes of his Southern master.

- "The Character of Man," inserted in autobiographical dictation 23 January 1906. Published in *Autobiography of Mark Twain, Volume 1* (University of California Press, 2010)

CHAPTER 1

Bill Yancey

.

All the Reasons to Trust Donald Trump

.

Bill Yancey

.

All the Reasons to Trust Donald Trump

.

Bill Yancey

.

All the Reasons to Trust Donald Trump

.

Bill Yancey

.

CHAPTER 2

Bill Yancey

.

All the Reasons to Trust Donald Trump

.

Bill Yancey

.

All the Reasons to Trust Donald Trump

.

Bill Yancey

.

All the Reasons to Trust Donald Trump

.

Bill Yancey

.

All the Reasons to Trust Donald Trump

.

Bill Yancey

.

All the Reasons to Trust Donald Trump

.

Bill Yancey

.

CHAPTER 3

Bill Yancey

All the Reasons to Trust Donald Trump

.

Bill Yancey

.

All the Reasons to Trust Donald Trump

.

Bill Yancey

.

All the Reasons to Trust Donald Trump

.

Bill Yancey

.

All the Reasons to Trust Donald Trump

.

Bill Yancey

.

.

Bill Yancey

.

CHAPTER 4

Bill Yancey

.

.

Bill Yancey

.

CHAPTER 5

Bill Yancey

.

.

Bill Yancey

.

All the Reasons to Trust Donald Trump

.

Bill Yancey

.

All the Reasons to Trust Donald Trump

.

.

Bill Yancey

.

.

Bill Yancey

.

CHAPTER 6

Bill Yancey

.

All the Reasons to Trust Donald Trump

.

Bill Yancey

.

.

Bill Yancey

.

All the Reasons to Trust Donald Trump

.

Bill Yancey

.

All the Reasons to Trust Donald Trump

.

.

All the Reasons to Trust Donald Trump

.

Bill Yancey

.

CHAPTER 7

Bill Yancey

.

All the Reasons to Trust Donald Trump

.

Bill Yancey

.

All the Reasons to Trust Donald Trump

.

Bill Yancey

.

.

Bill Yancey

.

All the Reasons to Trust Donald Trump

.

Bill Yancey

.

All the Reasons to Trust Donald Trump

.

Bill Yancey

.

All the Reasons to Trust Donald Trump

.

Bill Yancey

.

CHAPTER 8

Bill Yancey

.

All the Reasons to Trust Donald Trump

.

Bill Yancey

.

All the Reasons to Trust Donald Trump

.

Bill Yancey

.

All the Reasons to Trust Donald Trump

.

Bill Yancey

.

All the Reasons to Trust Donald Trump

.

Bill Yancey

.

.

Bill Yancey

.

CHAPTER 9

Bill Yancey

.

All the Reasons to Trust Donald Trump

.

Bill Yancey

All the Reasons to Trust Donald Trump

.

Bill Yancey

.

All the Reasons to Trust Donald Trump

.

Bill Yancey

.

All the Reasons to Trust Donald Trump

.

Bill Yancey

.

All the Reasons to Trust Donald Trump

.

Bill Yancey

.

CHAPTER 10

Bill Yancey

.

All the Reasons to Trust Donald Trump

.

Bill Yancey

.

All the Reasons to Trust Donald Trump

.

Bill Yancey

.

All the Reasons to Trust Donald Trump

.

Bill Yancey

.

.

Bill Yancey

.

All the Reasons to Trust Donald Trump

.

Bill Yancey

.

.

Bill Yancey

.

CHAPTER 11

Bill Yancey

.

All the Reasons to Trust Donald Trump

.

Bill Yancey

.

All the Reasons to Trust Donald Trump

.

Bill Yancey

.

All the Reasons to Trust Donald Trump

.

Bill Yancey

.

All the Reasons to Trust Donald Trump

.

Bill Yancey

.

All the Reasons to Trust Donald Trump

.

Bill Yancey

.

All the Reasons to Trust Donald Trump

.

Bill Yancey

.

CHAPTER 12

Bill Yancey

.

All the Reasons to Trust Donald Trump

.

Bill Yancey

.

All the Reasons to Trust Donald Trump

.

Bill Yancey

.

All the Reasons to Trust Donald Trump

.

Bill Yancey

.

All the Reasons to Trust Donald Trump

.

Bill Yancey

.

CHAPTER 13

Bill Yancey

.

All the Reasons to Trust Donald Trump

.

Bill Yancey

.

All the Reasons to Trust Donald Trump

.

Bill Yancey

.

All the Reasons to Trust Donald Trump

.

Bill Yancey

.

All the Reasons to Trust Donald Trump

.

Bill Yancey

.

All the Reasons to Trust Donald Trump

.

Bill Yancey

.

All the Reasons to Trust Donald Trump

.

Bill Yancey

.

All the Reasons to Trust Donald Trump

.

Bill Yancey

.

All the Reasons to Trust Donald Trump

.

Bill Yancey

.

CHAPTER 14

Bill Yancey

.

All the Reasons to Trust Donald Trump

.

.

All the Reasons to Trust Donald Trump

.

Bill Yancey

.

All the Reasons to Trust Donald Trump

.

Bill Yancey

CHAPTER 15

Bill Yancey

.

.

Bill Yancey

.

.

Bill Yancey

.

.

Bill Yancey

.

CHAPTER 16

Bill Yancey

.

All the Reasons to Trust Donald Trump

.

Bill Yancey

.

All the Reasons to Trust Donald Trump

.

Bill Yancey

.

All the Reasons to Trust Donald Trump

.

Bill Yancey

.

All the Reasons to Trust Donald Trump

.

Bill Yancey

.

All the Reasons to Trust Donald Trump

.

Bill Yancey

.

CHAPTER 17

Bill Yancey

.

All the Reasons to Trust Donald Trump

.

Bill Yancey

.

.

Bill Yancey

.

.

Bill Yancey

.

CHAPTER 18

Bill Yancey

.

All the Reasons to Trust Donald Trump

.

Bill Yancey

.

All the Reasons to Trust Donald Trump

.

Bill Yancey

.

CHAPTER 19

Bill Yancey

.

All the Reasons to Trust Donald Trump

.

Bill Yancey

.

.

Bill Yancey

CHAPTER 20

Bill Yancey

.

All the Reasons to Trust Donald Trump

.

Bill Yancey

.

All the Reasons to Trust Donald Trump

.

Bill Yancey

.

All the Reasons to Trust Donald Trump

.

Bill Yancey

.

CHAPTER 21

Bill Yancey

.

All the Reasons to Trust Donald Trump

.

Bill Yancey

.

.

Bill Yancey

.

All the Reasons to Trust Donald Trump

.

Bill Yancey

.

All the Reasons to Trust Donald Trump

.

Bill Yancey

.

CHAPTER 22

Bill Yancey

.

All the Reasons to Trust Donald Trump

.

Bill Yancey

.

CHAPTER 23

Bill Yancey

.

All the Reasons to Trust Donald Trump

.

Bill Yancey

.

All the Reasons to Trust Donald Trump

.

Bill Yancey

.

All the Reasons to Trust Donald Trump

.

Bill Yancey

.

CHAPTER 24

Bill Yancey

.

CHAPTER 25

Bill Yancey

.

All the Reasons to Trust Donald Trump

.

Bill Yancey

.

All the Reasons to Trust Donald Trump

.

Bill Yancey

.

.

Bill Yancey

.

All the Reasons to Trust Donald Trump

.

Bill Yancey

.

All the Reasons to Trust Donald Trump

.

Bill Yancey

.

CHAPTER 26

Bill Yancey

.

All the Reasons to Trust Donald Trump

.

Bill Yancey

.

All the Reasons to Trust Donald Trump

.

Bill Yancey

.

All the Reasons to Trust Donald Trump

.

The End

About The Author

Bill Yancey had the privilege of being the son of an air force officer and the grandson of an army officer. As a result, he lived all over the world, but never really grew up. He attended four high schools, a prep school, and five colleges. After bouncing out of an engineering curriculum, and spending time in Vietnam as a result, he finally obtained an undergraduate degree in general science from Virginia Tech in 1971. The Medical College of Virginia still regrets giving him an M.D. degree in 1976. He writes for his own entertainment, and hopes you see the humor in it, too.

Author's Statement

I have not asked my family or friends to read this book and/or put inflated reviews on the internet. I would appreciate it if you would put an honest review (good or bad) on the internet when you finish reading it. Even something as simple and short as, *I hated it*, *I loved it*, or *It was OK*, would be appreciated.

Also, you may contact me at: https://www. Goodreads .com/ You can direct comments or criticisms to me on my author page at that address. Thank you for spending your money and taking the time to read this novel. I hope you got your money's worth.

Sincerely,
Bill Yancey

Bill Yancey